Design Thinking for Beginners

Innovation as a factor for entrepreneurial success

by Kilian Langenfeld

Table of Contents

Introduction

In recent decades, there have been more inventions and innovations than ever before. Since 1980, the number of annual patents has tripled worldwide, reflecting the pressure on companies and organizations to innovate. Digitalization and growing globalization make it easy for new companies to be immediately present in the world market with a good idea. But where do companies get their new extraordinary and creative ideas from when they have outsourced innovation to a research department? No wonder no taxi company in the world has come up with a service like Uber because they didn't dare to think the impossible. But ideas are not born in an Excel document. Above all, however, it is often forgotten that people must be the focus of attention. The customer is not just a number in the accounting system but someone with needs that need to be met.

In medicine, it has been recognized that a new approach is needed to better understand diseases and people. This approach is holistic medicine, in which not only do the symptoms themselves play a role but also the medical history, the emotional state and the problems a patient has. The patient is simply viewed from different angles.

This approach is now also found in companies, under the term "Design Thinking". Anyone who wants to innovate today will hardly be able to avoid this method.

Just as a doctor cannot make a diagnosis alone, but is dependent on laboratories and X-ray specialists, so inventions and new ideas are not born in a small-roof chamber. Today, more than ever, innovation is teamwork.

David Kelley, who achieved fame founding his design and innovation agency "IDEO", has established Design Thinking in the economic sphere, which was previously only used in science. In addition, Professors Larry Leifer and Terry Winogard played a major role in the further development of Design Thinking in the American region. Design Thinking became even more central at the elite Stanford University through a specially founded institute, the so-called "d.school". The patron of the d.school was Hasso Plattner, the SAP founder.

In Germany, the School of Design Thinking was founded as part of the Hasso Plattner Institute, in cooperation with the "d.school" in Stanford. One can take a Basic Track and an Advanced Track and then dive far deeper into the subject than this little book is able to do.

Nevertheless, we want to give you an introduction to Design Thinking and help you to realize innovation projects with this method. Whenever there are problems that cannot be solved with conventional approaches, this method can be helpful.

Design Thinking: Definition

It should be noted that the term is already quite old because already in the late sixties L. Bruce Archer wrote in his book *Systematic Method for Designers* about a process he called Design Thinking. Robert McKim's later added "design engineering" to the term. In 1987, Peter Rowe published a book entitled *Design Thinking*, which at the time was still mainly aimed at architects and urban planners.

Today, Design Thinking is a method of solving problems in a practical and creative way. Unlike open brainstorming, this means that at the end of the process there must be a solution to a problem. This problem can be a problem that actually exists or one that is believed to arise in the future.

One example is the tourism industry: most large companies know that customers will eventually be able to book everything themselves—hotels, flights, excursions, guides, restaurants—and no longer need a travel agency. A Design Thinking process would try to find ideas for how to solve this problem of declining customer numbers.

Although Design Thinking can be described as an innovation process, you won't invent the next iPhone every time you participate in such a process. In this context, innovation means finding a new and unusual solution, an innovative solution.

There are two directions you can take when solving tasks:

- the problem-oriented direction or
- the solution-oriented direction

Bei der problemorientierten Lösung wird man vor allem analytisch vorgehen. Wie ein Wissenschaftler untersucht man zunächst das Problem, und versucht dann aufgrund der vorliegenden Informationen eine Lösung zu finden.

With the solution-oriented approach one tries to give in to approaching the goal, mostly by trying out, thus the classical "Trial and Error" principle. If the first idea doesn't work, you try the next one until you have found an acceptable solution.

In management circles, there is an interesting game that is often played at seminars and describes these approaches quite well: the participants have to build the highest possible tower out of dry spaghetti noodles, some tape and string as well as a marshmallow. Tom Wujec invented this game to show that our assumptions are often wrong, for example, that a marshmallow is very light and some spaghetti can it without breaking. It shows that you can't always solve problems with an analytical approach and that you usually only follow one approach. The aim of the game is to build the tower by trying it out as often as possible.

In Design Thinking there are several phases a process can go through, which will be described in a later chapter. But in order to get involved in such a process at all, you should know some basics and be able to fulfill some requirements.

What Is Design?

Understanding design is not about designing products or buildings. It's more about understanding the design process. How does a designer work? There is a saying—"form follows function"—in design and it describes quite well the fact that design is function-oriented or, even better, result-oriented. A design always solves a problem. If you have to build a new chair, you have to solve the problem that you have to sit well and comfortably on it or that new materials have to be processed cheaply. When you build a house, it has to satisfy certain ideas of the owners, for example an open fireplace and a hobby cellar. As a designer you will not start your architectural program and simply draw a floor plan. Instead, you will consider what feelings an open fireplace evokes or what ideas we associate with a hobby cellar. You will try to understand the world of the problem.

Design is also a visual process. Designers often work with prototypes, small models, photos or whatever material is at hand to materialize an idea. You can even get your Lego bricks out of the basement (or steal them from your children) and use them to build small prototypes.

Since this book is about Design Thinking and not design itself, we will leave it at this short definition. We'll come back to how design works in practice several times later.

Human-Centered Design (HCD)

In design, there is a school that places not only the solution to a problem but also the human being at the center of its efforts, at all stages of the design process. This is called "Human-Centered Design". Officially, HCD is described as follows in the corresponding ISO standard:

> *Human-Centered Design is an approach to developing interactive systems that aims to make systems meaningful and useful by focusing on users, their needs and requirements and applying factors such as ergonomics, knowledge and techniques. This approach improves efficiency, improves human well-being and user satisfaction, accessibility and sustainability. It also counteracts potential*

negative impacts on people, their health, safety and performance.[1]

Essentially, it forms the basis for Design Thinking because it is about the production of solutions and not just about a documentary process. Often the terms "Human-Centered Design" and "Design Thinking" are used together. The main difference is that Design Thinking has another focus. Human-Centered Design tries to improve the usability of a product by involving the user in the process. However, Design Thinking is more about creating products that meet a user's needs. There are interdisciplinary approaches and workshops but also an HCD approach. What both have in common is that they work iteratively. After pure teaching, Design Thinking has four phases and HCD six phases, but in practice these boundaries usually blur.

---

[1] International Organization for Standardization (2010): Ergonomics of human-system interaction -- Part 210: Human-centered design for interactive systems

Fields of Application

Before we dive into the process, the core of Design Thinking, we want you to get an idea of where you can use Design Thinking and where you can't. You can always use it when you want to create something new or when you want to solve a problem and need new and creative approaches. You will have to take care that Design Thinking is not the proverbial hammer that turns every problem into a nail. You can't solve everything with it, and in many areas Design Thinking just happens in parallel with or precedes a classic design and development process.

Sometimes these can be very small problems, such as the redesign of a hotel reception area. The reception halls always have the problem that they are large and spacious and the guest feels lost in them. They are often forced to walk a long way through this hall to the reception desk. With Design Thinking you can develop new ideas for how to solve this problem.

Let's assume that the reception area no longer complies with the new fire protection regulations because it needs another emergency exit. In this case you don't need any creative ideas, just good civil engineers who can check the statics and then decide where the exit should be built.

But you can also use Design Thinking to question internal processes and procedures in a company. For example, the management consultancy Roland Berger suggests anchoring this method as the basis for all decision-making processes in a company.[2]

A Design Thinking process does not replace concrete implementation. In the end there will always be a prototype, a model, which has to be programmed, manufactured or built.

---

[2] Roland Berger: Design Thinking: Von einer Produktentwicklungs-methode zu einem Ansatz für strategische Entscheidungsprozesse. URL: https://www.rolandberger.com/de/press/Design-Thinking-Von-einer-Produktentwicklungsmethode-zu-einem-Ansatz-f%C3%BCr-strate-2.html [Date of Reference: 20-04-2018]

Prerequisites

In order for a Design Thinking process to run success-fully, a number of prerequisites must be met. Man-agement in particular is required to meet these re-quirements and, above all, to provide the necessary resources. A Design Thinking process does not take weeks but can be carried out in a few short work-shops. However, it depends a little on how big the innovation project is and how extensive it is. Neverthe-less, the employees who are assigned to the project must also be available. If you are leading the project, you will have to insist that you get the people you need. Since Design Thinking is very interdisciplinary, you will sometimes have to do some persuasive work, such as why a warehouse employee should be in-volved in product innovation. But it is important that not only (or preferably not at all) the experts try to develop new and crazy ideas.

What you also need is time to do the process. It's no problem to spread it over several days, weekends or weeks, as long as you get the employees off for these events. Often it can happen that you also have to fight for it because such a workshop is not considered im-portant.

And this is especially true for the third condition: the attitude. Both the management and the participants in Design Thinking must be aware that there is no prohibition on thinking, that nobody is judged for their performance, and that it is an open-ended process. This means that at the beginning no one knows what the final result will look like. One only knows that one wants to work out a solution. Part of this attitude is that you don't need perfectionism, quite the contrary. The freer you are in your thinking, and the more you can improvise and build simple prototypes out of cardboard, the more likely you are to achieve a result.

The best way to ensure this is to get everyone involved and affected to get together before the Design Thinking process and explain what the project is about and what you want to achieve (and what you don't want to achieve). You will see at the end of the book why it is so important to have the right people on board and get as much support as possible when it comes to putting the idea into practice.

Processes

Design Thinking requires many different opinions and ideas, and these can and should always be revoked. It is up to a certain point a flowing process—like a river, which also has whirlpools again and again. At some point, a river has an end, but it's a long way to that point. Design Thinking can be based on three processes that are necessary to successfully implement the model.

Interdisciplinary

The interdisciplinary process means that during the different phases a team must be permanently diverse. Three engineers alone will not be able to achieve anything, just like three graphic designers. But if you put all six of them together and add a few other employees, something new can emerge.

However, teams are not always a harmonious group, especially when they are interdisciplinary and cross-departmental. But since the team is a fundamental part of the process, a small exercise follows to coordinate a new team.

Call the new team members together and have them write down answers to the following questions:

- What good experiences have I had in previous teams?

- What frustrated me a lot?

- What peculiarities do I have - for example, how do I do my work?

In the next step, the team sits down and everyone presents their answers. At first it's about getting to know each other better, but you can also extract rules from the answers, which then apply to the team. A good number are five rules. If everyone agrees, they are written down and declared as binding. The best way is to hang them up in the meeting room in the form of a large poster.

In the first few days, small ice breaker games can also help in the morning, especially when group exercises are called for. One is that you line up in a circle and everyone does not introduce themselves but the person next to them—not only by name but also by telling everyone something about the person.

In every team there will always be problems; that is in the nature of man. How can they be solved? By talking about them as early as possible. A creative process like Design Thinking needs all the power of the group, so disruptions should be fixed as soon as possible. The more open the communication in a group is, the better you will succeed. And such mediations are not necessarily the task of the team leader but of every team member.

A team leader can only lead his team if trust prevails. In Design Thinking, there should be no prohibitions on thinking, nor should anyone be afraid to say something wrong. The more trust a team leader and also the team members build among each other, the better they will be able to work together.

When putting together the team in the Design Thinking project, you should make sure that the participants have as different a background as possible. You are looking for people with ideas, not careerists who are always on the safe side. The less the participants have to lose, the crazier the ideas will be. Sometimes the helper from the cleaning service is a better choice than the creative personnel from the advertising department.

Iterative

Design Thinking is a non-linear model. There are no milestones, as in project management, which are processed one after the other. Instead, it is an iterative process in which you will and must go backwards again and again. Especially at the end of the phases there will be a prototype that will most likely go through the Design Thinking process again.

As with any good design, you're trying to find the solution by trying it out. Imagine building a house as big as possible out of playing cards. You will start with a small construction, but in the next step it turns out to be unsuitable, so you may have to create a new base that can carry more cards. That's how it will be in a Design Thinking process.

If you are used to doing classic project management, then the iterative steps are certainly a bit unusual. But if you have experience with the Scrum method, you will be able to handle it more easily. The iterative element runs through the whole project and all phases. You may need to rebuild prototypes (that's quite likely), but you may also need to rebuild individual phases or even the whole project. You wouldn't be the first to produce a good idea but it failed because certain parameters weren't known. The scaling of ideas always leads to problems and will force you to modify and adapt the ideas yourself.

Flexible

In creative processes, prohibitions on thinking are the worst thing that can happen. A boss who starts a Design Thinking project with the words, "Be creative, but please make sure you only use our own products, that the product is small, and that we can ship it soon," would have better said nothing because a design project has to be goal-oriented but also open to results. This means that at the beginning you have no idea what will actually come out at the end.

A historical example of this is the invention of the light bulb. Thomas Edison didn't have a brilliant idea and the next day the electric light was invented. In fact, he had to experiment a lot, try out new and other materials, question and understand how others did it and why it didn't work, until he finally had a carbon filament that glowed long enough and had the right voltage so it wouldn't burn right away.

Edison knew what he wanted but had to be flexible enough to try different materials. And even after he got the patent, he continued to work on improving the product.

If someone had told him that it was impossible to glow above a certain voltage, or if coal always crumbles into dust, we might not have any light today.

Flexibility in Design Thinking means that you have to be flexible in your thinking and question things over and over again.

Another example from this day and age is the Wiener Casino and the Lotteriezentrale[3]. For a long time, innovation here meant that the IT department was expected to come up with a proposal because today gambling almost exclusively takes place online, and you need a programmer for almost everything. There were indeed ideas, for example digital scratchcards, one of the big hits in German-speaking countries at online casinos. But that alone wasn't enough. So the entire company was rebuilt, there were new personnel assignments, there was a new interior and responsibil-

---

[3] Kramer, A. (2016): Design Thinking in der Praxis: Casinos, MAM, Erste Bank, ÖBB. URL:
https://www.trend.at/branchen/karrieren/design-thinking-praxis-7624507 [Date of Reference: 05-04-2018]

ities: Innovation is now a matter for the boss, the board has to ensure that new ideas are always produced. Another helpful feature was an "Awesome Challenge", in which teams of four people were to produce new ideas. And some useful approaches came to light, some of which will soon be implemented. Only because in this case the old habits were broken and innovation was placed on a somewhat more flexible and broader foundation had new ideas become possible.

Now you should know the essential basics to get into the Design Thinking process.

Phases

Design Thinking usually refers to phases that are passed through. It is quite common to go through these phases several times, and in some cases it is explicitly recommended. Even if these phases are often represented as a circle because they are not linear, they should be processed one after the other.

The phases are about approaching a solution slowly. In order to be biased as little as possible, one will first try to understand the situation in which one (and the customer/user) finds oneself. This is the immersion phase. The wider you do your research here, the more material you will have later when it comes to brainstorming. In the next phase you will analyze and organize the information that has been collected. It is about finding similarities and relationships. The next phase is the ideation phase, the part that is most fun because it is here that the ideas are sought (and hopefully found). This process can take some time because from the numerous ideas some particularly good ones have to be picked out. These are then used to build prototypes, either as objects or as concepts. The prototypes have to be tested in the end, until those are left that are believed to solve the problem best. Finally, you will have to put these ideas into practice.

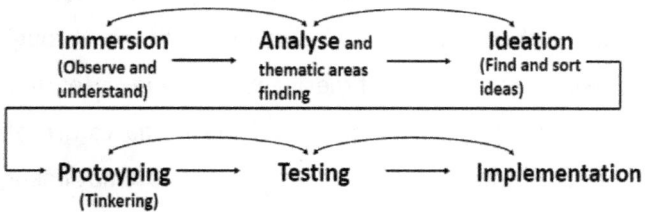

The arcs in the graphic should make it clear that the steps are connected and that you can go back again and again. Although the phases are sequential, they are mainly for logical reasons, so they are not necessarily to be understood as a linear sequence. Often Design Thinking is also represented as a circle to show that you can always go back to the beginning. But since it's about finding one or more solutions to a problem, we use the flow method here because there is definitely an end, namely the implementation phase.

However, it will rarely be the case that you jump from the immersion phase directly into the prototyping phase, at least not when you go through this process for the first time.

Immersion

The first phase is immersion. You are actually immersing yourself in the matter and the world of the problem. Sometimes this phase is also called the empathy phase.

The main purpose of immersion is to get into the customer's shoes and walk around in his world. This can even literally be the case with a shoe manufacturer: a manager would probably benefit from walking around in women's shoes with high heels for a whole day. But immersion doesn't just mean playing with your own products or trying them out. It's all about getting acquainted with customers (or employees) and their problems.

When renting Airbnb rooms, you require your employees to stay as Airbnb guests in different accommodations for a week after being hired. They should try out for themselves what the Airbnb customers experience, talk to them but also to the landlords, and learn how the world of Airbnb is designed. By the way, the background is a Design Thinking project: In the early days there were landlords but hardly any customers. In a workshop, the idea came up to hire professional photographers instead of using mobile phone photos taken by the landlords, who would then take higher quality pictures of the apartments. This paid off immediately, and the number of bookings rose rapidly. Even today, such a professional service is offered in the USA to ensure that real estate is actually put in the best light.[4]

The term empathy is often used in connection with Design Thinking and in the immersion phase you not only learn to understand how the customer thinks but also how he feels. Hotel surveys of customers are a good example: These always ask what their first impression was at the reception desk. However, it is often forgotten that the first impression is usually made by the security officer at the gate or in the parking garage. If this person has a friendly smile, the mood is much better than if a grouchy man is sitting there who does not feel like working. The same also applies to restaurants that offer a parking service or, for example, office buildings. The person who hears, "ID card," when entering a company building will not necessarily be in the best of spirits.

---

[4] Eshaghmohammadi, F. (2016): Become the patient – Design Thinking Grundlagen. URL:
http://www.ppcdetective.de/blog/design-thinking-blog/become-the-patient-design-thinking-grundlagen/ [Date of Reference: 15-05-2018]

The excursions are also about finding the so-called "extreme behaviors". Why does someone buy every shoe in a brand? Why does a product have so many comments online? Whether customers' experiences are positive or negative doesn't matter at first. More important is that you get many different opinions. The extreme points of view are so important because they will most likely lead you to new ideas later on.

Comprehension

In order to understand a problem, you have to examine it carefully. But you can hardly do that with the methods and tools that created the problem. The problem has mostly arisen in-house, and it is important to find out the history of the problem and how it is connected. This sounds more complicated than it is: Actually, you just have to collect all the information that has to do with the problem. The best way to do this is in small workshops. Let's assume that you have noticed that the sales department is not as efficient as it used to be, but you have no idea why. But because the competition is not asleep, something has to be done to make sales more efficient again.

First of all, you will talk to all employees involved in sales about how they perceive sales, what they think about employees and the sales system. You will want to know what assumptions are made about sales. You will then share these assumptions with everyone involved in the new sales project.

This process is also called "reframing". It is about you and the other employees being able to separate from the previous points of view and acquire new points of view.

If you work in tourism, or if you like to travel yourself, you will certainly have experienced that tourists complain about the fact that there are so many other tourists at the holiday resort. As outsiders we just shake our heads and think, *They are tourists themselves.* But as a traveler you have a different view of things and above all different expectations. Tourists often have a stereotypical picture of a holiday resort that is very close to a desert island with palm trees. When they come to a beach paved with hotels, they don't understand the world anymore. Your task in this case is to see the holiday resort through the eyes of the tourists but also to make their expectations your own. Also in this example you should not only make the customer journey yourself but above all have many conversations with tourists—your customers but also others—in order to understand what they expected.

It is often illuminating when you project all the results of the conversations you have had onto a pin board or as a mind map on the wall. By the way, mind maps are very suitable for this process, especially those that can be used collaboratively.

Observe

One method to better deal with the topic is to take part in excursions. Those who work in management particularly have little contact with the salesperson on the spot or with the customers who come into a business. But it can also be sufficient if you spend some time in a shopping mall where your company has a branch. Seeing and understanding the real world is an incredibly helpful process in Design Thinking and forms the basis for everything that follows.

The Bank of America once experienced this up close by simply talking to ordinary customers about how they use their normal checking accounts. They also came into contact with a woman who said that she pays her bills rounded up to the next dollar every month. On the one hand she didn't have the feeling that she owed any money to anyone, on the other hand at the end of the year she got back the extra money because she had paid too much, which made her happy. The bankers became sensitive and asked other customers not how much they were saving but why. And they found out that saving has an emotional component. So they turned the rounding up into a savings offer and the customers confirmed to them that it doesn't make much difference whether you save $10 or $100—the good feeling of having saved something is crucial. The bank received 700,000 new banknotes because it offered a kind of piggy bank account.[5]

Netflix can offer another example. They wanted to design a new interface there in 2011. As a rule, A and B versions of such software changes are created and then permanently tested with the help of users. They

---

[5] Russo, B. et al. (2012): Design Thinking Business Innovation, MJV Press, Rio de Janeiro

observed exactly what the users were doing. In the end, a new, denser version came out, which was criticized by many users. But it was used more and more intensively than the previous version. Bryan Gumm, a product developer from the USA, explained this experience in a nutshell: "What people say and what they do are rarely the same. We're not going to tailor the product experience just to please half a percent of the people."[6] (What people say and what they do is rarely the same. We won't change the product experience to only satisfy half a percent of customers.) That's why surveys are less appropriate, especially when you ask if something is good or not. Observing the user, on the other hand, does much more.

Nutella once proved that when Boris Becker was still an advertising figure. Becker had licked the Nutella from a knife in an advertising clip—something we all do. But there was an immediate outcry that this was dangerous for children. Nutella gave in and put a Nutella string player on the market that didn't have a sharp blade. What the example is supposed to show:

---

[6] Design for Founders: 10 Powerful Case Studies of Remarkable Business Growth With Design You Need to See. URL: https://www.designforfounders.com/business-growth-with-design/ [Date of Reference: 29-05-2018]

Nutella had simply understood that adults also like to eat it and that now—because they are adults—they can lick the knife to their heart's content without anyone scolding them. You only know such a thing if you observe exactly how the product is actually used and have an eye for details.

Going out

One rule is important for the excursions: the purpose is not to get confirmation of what you know or what you think you know. On the one hand it is important to listen, but on the other hand the exceptions to the rule—like the woman who rounds up—are especially important. One always finds something new where one normally does not search, in the corners—or statistically expressed, in the exception values. Where one normally neglects the outliers in a graphic, one looks closely at Design Thinking. For example, if you have a store that generates above-average sales, it's interesting to find out what happens there. The same also applies to stores that don't generate enough sales. In both cases, however, you should talk less to the local managing director than to the customers who come—or those passers-by who pass by the store.

Customer Trip

Another method is the customer journey: Live the life of a customer for one day and try to see where the so-called touch points are where a customer comes into contact with your company or service. An insulin syringe manufacturer wanted to know how to improve their product and had his employees live as diabetics for a day—including administering syringes themselves (but without insulin), monitoring food and checking glucose levels.

You can also use such a customer trip for many other products and services. Another example would be that you as a customer try to have your IT company develop a website. Even the role play itself will give you a lot of insights.

But it is not only about your company and your product itself. In order to understand the customer and his world, you must also observe his world. If your company is a clothing manufacturer, you will have to deal with trends. What importance does fashion have for your customers? What role models do they have? How do they decide what to wear in the morning? But also: Where can trendsetters be found? Which subcultures are there that fit fashionably to your products?

In this case you should just go to scene clubs and watch people. But you will also get similar impressions if you sit down at a lively place. Train stations and airports are always good places to go because there are many people there from different countries and social groups.

In sales, one often speaks of the five phases a customer goes through: Discovery of the problem ("I need new running shoes,"), information search ("What shoes are there? What do they cost? etc."), evaluation ("Which are cheaper? Which last longer?"), purchase decision ("I'll take these!"), behavior after the purchase ("Am I satisfied with the shoes?").

You can now get involved in every step of this process and ask questions. Paul Boag has written a fairly easy to understand article on how to start traveling with customers in his blog:

- What does the customer want to achieve in this step?

- What touch points are there in this step?

- How does the customer feel about this step?

- At what point do we lose the customer in this phase?

- Who or what influences the customer in this phase?

You can create a table from the questions and steps, which can then serve as a frame. It's better than just entering keywords, it is also better to use pictures or drawings to get a stronger visual representation.

Recording

But how can you even record the many experiences you have outside?

The easiest way is using videos and photos but also numerous handwritten notes. You can also use the recording function of your mobile phone to conduct small interviews, which you can then either summarize or transcribe later.

In the observation phase it is important to collect as much different information as possible without distorting it with guiding questions. They must be as raw and honest as possible.

The **recording work** may not be as interesting as observing itself, but it is very important for the project. No matter how good your memory is, you will have forgotten your observations by the time you return to the workshop. The best thing is to decide in advance how you want to process the information, whether there is a digital format or whether it should be written down on paper. You can also make small index cards (see examples below) that can later make sorting on a wall easier.

Desk Work

There may be employees who don't want to go out. That's no problem because you can also find out what your customers think from your desk. This is where **digital observation** comes in. As a customer, try to find out what other customers think about your product or service. Of course, it is easiest to read the comments on your Facebook page again or to research the company blog and other social channels. But you can also search for your product in the search engines and check if there are any reviews, if someone has written something about it, or if there are basically reviews. A recommendable place is still the good old forums, which are still very popular, especially in Germany. Choose forums that are thematically close to your product.

It is also important here that you only observe. There's a great temptation to reply to a forum post or a Facebook comment, but that's not your job. You can copy the link and forward it to Customer Service if there is a problem. But you're just a squirrel collecting nuts (but not hiding them!).

To come back to the tourism example: Here you can browse through wonderful travel blogs. You will read in many travelogues that travelers were either excited "that it was just us and the locals," or that they complained "because there were Chinese everywhere and then also the American groups."

Analysis

You've collected a lot of information now, and it's all in a digital or real folder or both. Now it's time to understand this data. And for that they have to be removed from the folder and made visible. The best way is to use a wall to which you can attach everything you can have on paper. Videos and audio contributions can be visualized with placeholders and a small description.

Most Design Thinking teams use such a wall or large blackboard because the haptic experience and physical presence of objects usually stimulates creativity more strongly and you have the same image in front of you. You can also use electronic mind maps or similar, especially for smaller projects. At team meetings it is best to use a projector to throw this mind map visibly onto the wall.

> **Caution:** Diversity, teamwork and out-of-the-box thinking are required in all phases of Design Thinking. That is why it is important that the sorting of the observation material is ideally carried out together.

In the first step, everything is simply glued to the wall as it comes. Think of it as a suitcase that you empty after a journey. You just tip it out and see on the floor the dirty laundry, the souvenirs, the shell from the beach and the practical elastic trousers that you wore every day but would never put on here.

Just as you start by looking at your empty suitcase, separating things according to holiday memories and what comes back to everyday life (wash bags, clothes, shoes, hair dryer), you will now also start sorting your collected observations.

Sorting

Once everything has been emptied and placed on the wall in a clearly visible position, it is time for sorting. The so-called insight cards, as recommended, for example, by the American company IDEO, which is one of the pioneers in Design Thinking, can help here.[7]

Actually these are simple index cards, which are all structured uniformly, for example as follows:

Title	
Description	
Source	

---

[7] Design Kit: Methods. URL: http://www.designkit.org/methods [Date of Reference: 01-06-2018]

Using the example of a textile manufacturer, a map of an excursion could look like this:

Title	Nonsensical inscriptions "Man Bike ATM."
Description	People wear T-shirts with letter-ing that doesn't make sense as if they were made by chance.
Source	Observation at XX.XX. at station Y.

If you did an online search, the map would look like this:

Title	Black bleaches out.
Description	Customers complain that the color of the black blouse quickly bleaches out.

Source	http://abcdefg.com

You can actually use such maps already during the observation phase, but there are also advantages if the first observations are as raw as possible and then summarized on the maps.

Such maps can also be provided with photos. In the context of videos, a card should describe the content of the video briefly.

Categorize

Now you have it a little easier to look at the different observations, and it is time to find similarities. It's best to have all the team members stand in front of the wall and everyone can give their opinion about which cards belong together or are related to each other. You can also make this visible by using different colored strings to connect the cards.

The most important question you and your team need to ask when sorting cards is: Why? Why do people like funny labels? Why is fading such a problem (OK, the answer is obvious, but why do they write in the forum and not directly to your company)? You will have to try to figure out what drives your customers, what their needs are.

Good keywords to use to search are:

- behavior
- wishes
- dreams
- reality
- needs
- responsible persons

- contact persons

In the English Design Thinking literature one speaks of users, needs and insights that belong together. This means that you start from the contents of the cards to identify certain types that have certain needs, as you found out in your observations.

> **Caution:** It is expressly not a question of finding the lowest common denominator! Rather, the focus is on better understanding the needs and making them visible, and there is not just one need among your customers.

The goal is to define a so-called point of view (POV)—a kind of micro-theory about the problem area and the needs of the users. The way to this POV includes several subprocesses: The team starts with storytelling, i.e. the research findings are shared within the team. These insights are then grouped by topic to identify patterns. During synthesis, these insights are grouped into a visual framework (such as a two-by-two matrix, a Venn diagram, or a causal map) or a user-related person (which can be a character profile, a customer trip, or a usage scenario). This is then transformed into the point of view, which is a usually verbalized (sometimes metaphorical) description of the specific problem identified and contains a micro-theory about the user's needs.

There are hundreds of different ways to sort something, from chronological sorting to alphabetical sorting to factual sorting. But it is better if you find a common framework for certain observations. The example of tourists would be the following observation:

> "Travelers expected to find a pristine landscape, not tourists."

> But what is important for you is behind this statement: "Tourists want an authentic experience and not other tourists."

You have already found a problem with this and consequently also possible solutions—namely to bring tourists to places where there are no other tourists (which may be a bit difficult in Paris or at the pyramids in Egypt, but that is the challenge).

If you work with mind maps, you don't have to create a vertical structure, you can work horizontally, which gives you more space and a better overview. The analysis phase is all about identifying problems and possible solutions or challenges.

With all the information you and your team have collected, you can now make a small sub-map for each insight card. On this card you make a note:

- What satisfies the observer?
- Why does it satisfy him?
- What doesn't the observer like?
- Why doesn't he like it?

Small Signposts

While there are no restrictions on collecting the information, it can happen that some of the data you have received does not fit the project at all. For example, when it comes to the expectations of tourists at the holiday destination, the complaints about the food on the plane are second or even third.

To make sure that there are no losses of important information and that the collection does not fray, you can set up small signposts. If you are working on a large wall, you can paint it on the sides, but you can also build small cardboard signs that show the way to the wall. For example, you can place them on the wall:

→ We want to offer the best experience to our guests

→ We want to go new ways in tourism

→ We want to communicate better with our customers

These guidelines are based on the one hand on the project itself (solutions for customer complaints); on the other hand they will also crystallize from the data itself. Ideally, one person on the team should keep an eye on these little signposts and possibly update them as well.

Caution: It is sometimes difficult to determine whether a piece of information is something trivial or an extreme view. The latter is actually what you're looking for, so you should always reassess before putting an insight card aside.

Defining the Needs

The team should now be at a point where the fog clears a bit and you can already see a piece of the sky. You now have a more concrete idea of what customers want, what the problem is, and what opportunities it offers. But in many cases this is still too general and above all not really tangible.

There are several methods to help you better understand whether your information really reflects the needs of users—one of which is the SPICE method.

This stands for **Social, Physical[8], Identity, Communication and Emotional**. It describes a framework in which the needs of users can be determined and represented. Your task is to find out the hidden needs of customers or users, those that cannot be satisfied so far.

One example is refrigerators: they are something we all have in the kitchen that we absolutely need. But they are usually ugly, clunky and take up a lot of space. Buyers of refrigerators don't just want a functional appliance; they also want one that satisfies their desire

---

[8] Design Thinking: The Guidebook for Public Sector innovation in Bhutan. URL: http://www.rcsc.gov.bt/wp-content/uploads/2017/07/dt-guide-book-master-copy.pdf [Date of Reference: 20-06-2018], S. 28

for a well-equipped kitchen.[9] As part of a Design Thinking process, one kitchen manufacturer finally came to the conclusion that kitchen appliances are more and more a piece of furniture and are also regarded as such. That's why we stick magnets on our refrigerators or use them as note holders.

So the customers' need would have been: "I want the fridge to fit in with the overall interior because I want my home to be beautifully furnished."

But SPICE can also help to understand the customers and their deeper needs. Such needs are usually formulated in more general terms, for example: "I want to save money," or, "I want to live healthy." It can also be behaviors like, "I want to be alone," or, "I don't like to be alone," "I like places I already know," or, "I like to explore new things."

These needs are usually social ("I value what my friends think"), emotional ("I feel good eating chocolate") or physical ("exercise reduces my stress").

---

[9] Gullberg, G.; Widmark E.; Nyström, M.; Landström, A. (2006): DESIGN THINKING in BUSINESS INNOVATION

In order to bring together the findings from both the information collection and the needs analysis, you can visualize them. An old marketing technique, the persona, helps here.

Personas

Personas are ideal types of a customer. While one normally tries to understand the customer as the average of all data, one goes with the personas another way. First of all you have to understand that there is not only one type of customer or employee. Just because 60 percent of customers are female doesn't mean you only have to produce for women. Just because 40 percent like to order noodles and only 20 percent rice doesn't mean that there are only noodles left. Instead, in this case one tries to imagine both the rice and the noodle friend better.

Let's take the example of wanting to improve the canteen in the company. Fewer and fewer employees use the canteen, and there are complaints about the menu. You have talked to many employees, the kitchen team and guests, searched the company's intranet for comments, and your team has already produced a comprehensive map with all the information and categories. This also leads to a war of inserts, among other things. It turns out that in addition to the noodle and rice factions, there is also a potato faction, and also the low-carb friends who do not want any side dish. But it also turns out that potato and pasta eaters are more likely to change than rice eaters. It is therefore important to better understand the rice eater.

A persona should represent the needs of the customer, his motivation and his expectations. In marketing, one also tries to use many outward appearances, such as gender, income, education, purchasing power and the like. But Design Thinking is all about the soft factors.

You can give these people names, like "Max" or "Rita", but it is better to name them after an outstanding characteristic, like "travel eater".

A persona is then described in this way:

Max likes to eat rice because he believes that rice is healthier and has fewer calories. He wants to maintain his weight. He also finds it easier not to eat rice completely. Max also eats little meat and likes to go to farmers' markets. He spends most of his holidays in Asia, where he cycles a lot. He works in bookkeeping.

> **Caution:** The personas are fictional persons, not really existent. They are put together like a construction kit from the information that often describes extremes.

You should have four to seven different personas depending on the project, but even these numbers are not carved in stone. Most of the time your info wall will give you the number of personas, if you have sorted the information well enough. In any case, you should discuss with the team who these personas can be.

Some design thinking seminars teach that you can make a persona like a passport, with a kind of photo, name and description. This is a good way to visualize the persona, but it should be at the end. It is better to distinguish the different personae by their behavior or desire and then build an ideal type around them. In other words, the personae do not distinguish age and gender but why they do something or why they like to do something.

You can create a profile for the different people:

Briefing	Name:	
Age: Sex: Place of residence: Occupation: Education: Income: Family:	Goal: Motivation:	Inner needs:
Hobbies: He/she likes to do: Dislikes:	Challenges:	External needs:
Living environment:	Behavior:	

Ideation

The next step is probably the most important in Design Thinking. But it is also the most exciting. The term ideation comes from the English word idea, and this is exactly what we are talking about here. It's the process of finding ideas. When a designer wants to design a new chair, he will first look at what other chairs look like and talk to people about what they want from a chair and how they use it. Some sit relaxed leaning back, others even put a foot up, and still others need armrests. Only after this phase can the designer sit down at the drawing table and begin to put ideas on paper.

It's similar with Design Thinking for other processes. It's now about solving the problems you've identified. You want to help the personas you've developed. Or to stick with our example: It's about satisfying both rice and pasta lovers in the canteen or giving tourists a more valuable experience in their destination country.

The best thing to do now is to take on the personas again because they most likely symbolize your problem. Now it's time to think about how you can solve the person's problem. You write down the needs and ask what the solution looks like. For example:

> *How can we fulfill Max's desire for more Asian and healthy food?*

> *How can we also make him taste potatoes?*

These are already concrete questions and the answers should be just as concrete now, the best way to do it again is to use a blackboard or a wall to which notes are stuck.

Methods of Brainstorming

You probably already know one method to find ideas: good old brainstorming. This also happens here, with some special features. So it is important that as many different participants as possible are involved. Most books and seminars even require designers to be present because that's what the interaction between designers and analysts is all about. Now, there are industries in which nothing is designed but in which services are very well developed as products.

It's not so much about the title of the brainstorming members but about the fact that they all have different backgrounds. Now the problems are presented to them and then we can think about it. Sometimes it all works by itself, especially if the brainstormers have some experience with this procedure. However, if you have a group in front of you that might have some difficulties getting started, you can also help a little. One way is the three-way method.

Triple Method

Each participant receives a sheet of paper consisting of three columns and three rows. Each participant can enter up to three ideas in the first row. Then the sheet is passed on, and now the ideas that are already there must be further developed and improved.

You can vary the rows and columns according to the number of participants. It should be clear to everyone that it is about ideas that have to do with the question but also that they can be free in what they think. Often people have an inhibition in their minds because they are afraid of doing something wrong. That would be fatal in this process. So you have to try to encourage everyone to present crazy ideas. What is not possible in the end will be sorted out anyway. So if you think you can offer tourists a unique experience where they don't see any other tourists by shooting them to the moon, you can write that down. Maybe another participant will make something more realistic out of it, like a NASA simulator or a virtual moon journey. It is important that such suggestions are made.

But the sheets are only one way to get ideas. Another is to get on the ground. The participants will be divided into groups of four, and a very large sheet of paper (A1, A0 or even larger) will be placed on the floor. Now they get either a box with photos showing all sorts of things or a box with different toy figures. You can organize the toys beforehand by bringing some from everyone who has children. You can also use Lego or other building blocks. It's not so much about what these objects represent as about making associations. This prevents everyone from staring at an empty sheet of paper and no ideas coming up.

If you want it to be more formal, you can also hold so-called co-creation meetings. These are especially suitable for smaller groups of up to 10 people. You sit down and start with small ideas that don't necessarily have to do with the project. It's all about getting your brain going.

A simple question is: What do we need to bake a cake? There it will be bubbling with proposals because almost everyone can contribute something to it. But you will also be able to identify participants who are calmer and possibly support them.

> **Attention:** Some participants will refuse such support and say they are simply not a creative person. But anyone can be creative, only this creativity needs to be led into an activity.

In brainstorming sessions, the mistake is often made that they are led by an executive in the company. This is not a good idea for group dynamic reasons because employees think they have to perform well. It is also of little help to point out that everyone can think freely. If your head of department wants to be part of a team, then he should become part of a team like everyone else.

In fact, brainstorming doesn't need real leadership, it just needs someone to look at the clock, hand out materials and help if someone (or a whole group) doesn't move forward.

Sometimes it is better not to brainstorm in the company itself but to go outside. However, this should not be a neutral and sterile hotel meeting room but something that inspires. If the weather permits, you can also simply go to a meadow or a park. When it rains, it can be a co-working space or a coffee shop offering large tables. If you want to think "out of the box", you should also be physically outside the box, if that is possible.

SCAMPER

SCAMPER is a brainstorming technique that provides fairly good results, especially with physical objects and products. It stands for:

S - Substitutes (What can be replaced?)

C - Combine (What can I combine with it?)

A - Adapt (What does this remind me of?)

M - Modify and Magnify (How can I change it?)

P - Put to other use (What else can I do with it?)

E - Eliminate (What can I do without the object? What can I take away?)

R - Reverse (What happens if I use it the other way round?)

Usually the participants are given an object in their hands because brainstorming works best when many senses are addressed simultaneously. You can then write the letters one below the other on a flip board, and the team members can write down their ideas in the horizontal column. This method also generates a large number of ideas, but it also has the advantage that they are already categorized.

Creating Analogistic Inspiration

You can also bridle the horse from behind when it comes to inventing a different approach. And so you can take a look at other industries, for example, and find out how they solved these problems. Often enough, we only learn from companies that do essentially the same thing, rather than from those that do something completely different but face the same problems.

The analogistic inspiration works quite simply:
The team members get studies from other industries and companies that show how innovation is understood and implemented there. On a large wall (or blackboard), after reading the studies, participants can write on small pieces of paper what positive experience they have had. This can also be several ideas per study. First, all the notes are glued randomly. When everyone is ready, the notes are to be summarized thematically.

Convergence

No matter which method you use, try to get many, and above all many different, ideas. Crazy ideas in particular are always welcome, and ideas should not be discussed in the brainstorming process. Even the next step, convergence, is not about the quality of the idea. Rather, it is about placing the ideas in topic areas. They have to be sorted.

Here, too, the whole team should work together. You look at the ideas together and then suggestions should be made, which superior terms might fit for some ideas.

Let's say you've been looking for ideas to improve the canteen. Suggestions came such as ordering online, vegan food, higher quality tables and chairs, rice and noodles as a side dish, takeaway food, cooking workshops and much more.

The topics could then be as follows:

> Menu - What to eat?
>
> Infrastructure - Furnishing, Counter, Opening hours
>
> Digitalization - Online order, Website with calorie data
>
> Actions - Cooking courses, Theme weeks

Such clusters are the first step of categorization, but they can also be changed. Also, the discussion about the topic areas should not last too long and should not take an academic direction. It helps to call up the basic problem again and again. The canteen example is about improving the acceptance of the canteen, i.e. ultimately about attracting more employees to the canteen again.

This is where the first difficult decision comes in: You will have to decide on a few clusters, those that seem promising to you. We will then continue to work with them. But how do you know which clusters are the right ones? You don't. That's what makes Design Thinking so appealing. You don't throw away the other clusters, you leave them behind. If the topic fields you have selected turn out to be wrong, you can simply go back and use the other topic fields. That's the heart of Design Thinking: That you try, test and then start all over again.

Practical example: Melina Costa, who owns the innovation consultancy Coaeva, was commissioned by the Adalbert Raps Foundation to design a new, innovative concept for butchers. The butchers had to contend with considerable declines in turnover, on the one hand due to Creutzfeldt-Jakob disease, which could be transmitted by cattle brains, and on the other hand due to cheap supermarkets. The butcher's trade is also a very traditional trade and therefore not the spearhead of innovation. In discussions with many companies, it turned out that the partners of the butchers often cooked small dishes, which the customers then either ate at the bar table or even took home with them. The students from the Hasso Plattner Institute who were involved in the project therefore had the idea that small lunch boxes could be offered. These should contain a meat dish but also something to drink and perhaps even a small dessert. They then had several butchers make prototypes. The result was a disaster: greasy escalopes on soaked rolls, an orange juice drink and a Hanuta slice. It seemed as if the butchers either didn't understand what it was about or didn't feel like collaborating. And indeed the latter was the case. They did not want innovation; they only wanted an appreciation of craftsmanship. They went back to the observation phase and added the butchers themselves as a group whose needs were to be observed. As a result, the problem was no longer called "How to modernize a business" but "How the butcher's trade remains relevant." In the end, there was the truffle hunt project, in which the butchers visited the particularly innovative companies and themselves explained what they did differently. Many were given ideas that they implemented, but what was most heard was that the butchers were "proud again to be butchers."

The example is intended to illustrate that a process in Design Thinking is not linear and that one usually only notices towards the end of the ideation phase or in the prototype phase that one is on the wrong path.

So once you've found your subject areas, it's time to select ideas to pursue. Here, too, the other ideas are kept because you might still need them later (and a few Post-its are hardly going to take up any space).

Reconciliation

Since there are probably still a lot of ideas contained in the topic fields, it can be very time-consuming to discuss which of them should be further developed. The simplest method is good old voting. Everyone has one vote and the ideas with the most votes win. You should also try this with a small team because in the end it is all about making a decision in this phase. Whether this is right or wrong will then turn out, and actually there are no right or wrong decisions in Design Thinking. Your mission is to solve a problem, not to write an academic paper on different approaches.

Not only do you have to further develop the winner of the vote, but you can also, depending on the scope of the ideas, take several suggestions into the next phase. Usually this is the better way because you can learn from each other when realizing several ideas and save some time. Of course, there is not only one solution for a problem but many different solutions that can be implemented differently quickly and easily.

You can also differentiate the vote a bit by creating three categories in which each has a vote. You can use this as an example: The easiest idea to implement, the best fitting idea and the craziest idea. This ensures that not only is mediocrity still used but also exceptional approaches are pursued.

Building Prototypes

An idea is not worth much if it is only written on paper. Only if you try to realize it can you can see if it can really solve the problem you have identified—or if it works at all. A prototype is the visualization of an idea. But now it depends very much on your project what such a prototype can look like. The simplest ideas are always those that can somehow be made physically visible. When it comes to setting up the company headquarters, you can work with shoe boxes and doll-house furniture to define certain areas. For example, in the new Apple headquarters, they deliberately distributed quite a few toilets in the circular building to force employees to walk through the corridors and meet other employees they might not otherwise meet. You can make this visible in a prototype. In the canteen example, you can indeed cook a vegan dish or build a quick-and-dirty website that contains the essential elements of the idea for online ordering.

Mostly prototypes have different degrees of realization or abstraction; that's why we talk about abstract and concrete prototypes.

In the case of abstract prototypes, the implementation of the idea is usually represented as a concept. In the case of concrete prototypes, a model is built.

Abstract Prototypes

In order to turn an idea into a concept, a little more focus is needed. What was the width during brainstorming is now being narrowed. The concept should clearly and unambiguously explain how the customer's needs are to be solved and which advantages he has from solving the problem.

You can either take the persona again or—if you haven't done it yet—try to understand the customer experience to see where your concept can best start.

Try to introduce the customer to you and think about how and when he will come into contact with your product or service. It's similar to customer travel, but now you're not observing so much, you're taking on the role of the persona and trying to empathize with their needs.

In the example of the canteen, for example, the customer experience already begins at work when you ask yourself what you want for lunch. The next step is the canteen's website. Then the customer comes to the canteen itself and gets a tray. What's the experience on the way to the issuing points? When and where does he see the daily menu? How and where can he find a free table?

Try to imagine all these steps, write them down and think about where your idea can best start. Remember the example of the tourists who don't want to see other tourists. Let's assume that one idea is to offer them, after they have booked their trip and the hotel, an extra excursion where they can explore the untouched areas and surroundings of the city they are flying to. When is the best time to offer them this? When they book your trip? Or when you send them the travel documents? Or when they have landed? Or after they have checked into the hotel?

In most cases, the problem will not arise until the tourists have checked in and visited the area. Maybe they won't know how busy it is until the next day. This is the best time to get in touch with them and make them an offer for the trip.

If you wanted to sell them the trip at the time of booking, they might see it as an aggressive sales tactic. An exception, however, would be when it comes to addressing experienced customers as a target group. They already have the problem at the time of booking, so you can make them the offer of the excursion exactly at this point.

This process may sound banal, and is logical for some marketing experts even without further explanation. But this is only the case because after you have understood personas and their experiences, you are, of course, always smarter. In other words, if the marketing department knew all of this, you wouldn't have to do a Design Thinking workshop.

You won't make revolutionary inventions with Design Thinking, and many of the ideas are copied and already exist in a similar way. But that's not the point. It's just about finding ideas that solve a problem. You shouldn't forget that. Design Thinking is not a competition for ideas but a method to solve customer problems.

Once you know which idea would best fit where in the customer experience, you can start formulating the concept. This can be a description of the excursions in the example of tourism and the process of how to bring them to the customers (representative in the hotel or by email?), in the example of the canteen it could be the rough design of an intranet site.

Concrete Prototypes

If your project is about developing a product, it should be visualized as much as possible. But as far as possible, this doesn't mean that you have to finish the complete product right at the beginning.

Example: A bank wanted to know how they could improve their ATMs. They found out that customers perceive the machine first as a machine then as an interface and as a room. So it played a role that you could hear the rattling of the banknote dispensing roll because customers are always afraid that they are doing something wrong and then they don't get any money. As soon as they heard the rattling, they felt relieved. So with the prototype it was important to avoid turning off the rattling noise, even though it doesn't sound high-tech at all. In the Design Thinking workshop,

ATMs were built out of cardboard; the rattling was simulated with a toy car engine. But they also built some without the corresponding noise to test if this was really important. It turned out already at the cardboard model that customers missed something.

One method, by the way, was to build a cardboard frame, and one team member simply "played" the ATM while another represented the customer.

Another good example was the development of children's toothbrushes. IDEO had looked into the subject and found that children hold toothbrushes differently from adults. They do not yet have pronounced fine motor skills, and, like a fork or a spoon, they cling to the toothbrush with their whole hand. As a prototype, they simply wrapped paper around a normal toothbrush and found that this was enough to make it easier for the children to brush their teeth. The children's toothbrush developed from this was the best-selling in the USA, and since then almost all toothbrush manufacturers have copied this concept.[10]

---

[10] Lanoue, S. (2015): IDEO's 6 Step Human-Centered Design Process: How to Make Things People Want. URL:

The developers of IDEO are known for working mostly with cardboard and simple materials when it comes to building prototypes. And that they are successful can already be seen in the products they have helped to develop, including the first computer mouse for Apple, the Palm Pilot and a mechanical whale for the film *Free Willy*.

With a prototype, you should never make it too complicated. IDEO's motto is: "How can I do something with a minimum of time to get feedback from the users as quickly as possible?"

Should the User Already Be Involved in the Prototype?

The question as to whether the users should also be part of the team, or whether they can at least help to develop the prototype, is a matter of opinion. Some think that the process of Design Thinking is user-oriented but does not involve it. Others say that the user cannot be involved early enough. The best thing is probably a middle ground. In the beginning, it would probably be more harmful if the customers constantly

https://www.usertesting.com/blog/2015/07/09/how-ideo-uses-customer-insights-to-design-innovative-products-users-love/ [Date of Reference: 10-05-2018] made comments while observing. Especially with projects within a company this can be really disturbing. But there's no reason why users shouldn't be involved right from the prototype development stage. Since they are needed for testing anyway, you can integrate them a little earlier. The only important thing is not to form a test group out of it.

Testing

As soon as the first prototype is ready, the next step is to test it. The earlier it can be tested, the better. Testing is not about seeing if a prototype works but about how the idea is received by the customer. First, you want to get basic feedback. Assuming IDEO had built the children's toothbrush prototype with a square-shaped timber, the children would probably have said it hurt to hold on to it. With a model ATM that doesn't clatter when you spend money, that would also be noted. With a canteen website, the first impression would be "Where is the dish of the day?"

Test Groups

One of the difficult tasks in Design Thinking is to find suitable test groups. The team members drop out because they are too much involved in the process. If the project is supposed to solve a problem that exists within the company, then it is best to select employees who are directly affected. Try to get as mixed a group as possible rather than as large a group as possible. You want to hear a lot of different opinions first; the last thing you want is someone patting you on the back out of collegiality.

If customers are the users of the prototype, then you can proceed as with focus groups and invite them to a small workshop. Usually it's not enough to sit in a circle with them and show them the prototype. Some Design Thinking experts even say that proper testing and the associated process are crucial to the end result.

So you should think carefully about what you want to test and how users will use it. If you have developed a simple prototype, try to make several copies at once so that the workshop participants don't have to wait. At the beginning of the test you should explain what the project is about, what you learned in the observation phases, what problem you identified and how you want to solve it. This should not be an hour-long PowerPoint presentation but just a brief introduction to the workshop. The more playfully the prototype can be handled, the better. It doesn't matter if the cardboard model might fall apart. The first tests are about the basic idea.

Your task and that of the team during testing is to listen carefully and above all to take a lot of notes. Especially at the beginning, a formal process with questionnaires would be a hindrance, so it is necessary to write down comments. Theoretically, the workshop can also be recorded on video, but some clients are bothered by cameras and in the end someone has to write down what they say anyway.

The notes should first be assigned to the customers but then divided into subject areas. Now it's no longer about finding new ideas but about looking at how you can improve the product or prototype.

Caution: Failure is part of testing. This is the only way you can make the prototype better. There are exceptions, however, where the prototype fails to its full extent so that the whole project can be questioned. That happens, but the big advantage of Design Thinking is that you can find it out very early and save a lot of development costs.

Living with the User

The test phase is another empathy phase because here you have to understand again how the user or customer feels, how he thinks, and how he understands and uses the product. Testing is not about whether the target group likes the product or not. It's about knowing why they like it—or why not. Or even better: What they like and what they don't like and why.

This also includes having the tester actually tested. If he or she has questions, you are welcome to answer them, but otherwise you should see how they are dealt with and above all ask questions about feelings and sensitivities. Especially with products that can be handled, such emotional approaches play a greater role than the actual functionality.

What you should avoid is something to explain during testing. If someone opens the flap of a new bread can the wrong way round, there's probably a design flaw, otherwise it wouldn't happen. At least let it happen, even if the lid is torn off—that's why you built a cheap prototype.

If time and team size allow, you can give users several prototypes to solve the problem and then have them compare. This works especially well with abstract prototypes: Here you can very easily change the colors or the arrangement on a website, or just have three or four different versions to choose from. This is often applied to a new app, which is then sent to test users. Here the test groups are mostly divided, where group A gets beta version 1 and test group B gets beta version 2 and so on.

Digital Testing

When the product or service is digitized, you can also collect a lot of useful data. Particularly when it comes to functionality, you can quickly send out new prototypes and have them retested. You can also use the data to see how an app is used, which pages of a website are opened, and how and whether a test purchase is carried out. But for digital products you should define an exact test process. This also includes which data should be recorded and evaluated. Such data can be:

- Dwell time in the app

- Dwell time per page

- How many interactions were made?

- How often per day/week was the app/page used?

- When was the feedback sent (after a complete test or in between)?

- Which functions have been tried and which not?

Despite the amount of data you can collect, you should also try to have real conversations with digital products. There are certainly some users in your environment that you can invite (at this point again the note: No friends, no family, and no colleagues). Even a single hour with real people can sometimes bring more than a week of digital testing.

Finding and Understanding Errors

After the first test round you will have received a lot of comments. These have to be sorted and understood. In most cases there will be three main categories:

- Functional errors

- Errors that only partially solve the problem

- Errors in understanding the problem

With the functional bugs you can again distinguish between those caused by the limited functionality of a prototype (which you still have to fix) and those that functionally hinder the problem solving. With an electric toothbrush, for example, this would be an on/off button in the wrong place that is accidentally touched.

It may also be that a problem is only partially solved. In the case of ATMs, for example, the angles of the displays had been improved so that they were easy to read even when the sunlight was different. However, this meant that people of a certain size had difficulties reading the display. Nobody in the development group had been big enough, so the problem didn't arise until the prototype was tested (an iPad had been used for demonstration).

If there are errors in the understanding of the problem, then it quickly becomes apparent in the prototype. And this happens very often. The reason is usually that you didn't observe and learn enough and accepted a problem that might not even exist. That's what happened with Coca-Cola, for example. In 1985, the idea of having to change the composition and bring the new Coca-Cola onto the market somehow came up. Nobody had asked for it, and therefore nobody wanted this new product. The company rowed back. By the way, Pepsi had a similar disaster with Crystal Pepsi. Again and again large companies have developed products to the end only to find that customers simply don't like them. Apple's Newton Tablet was not even liked by Steve Jobs (not least because it had a stylus he hated), and Segway vehicles today are actually only found at security services in shopping malls and spas.

Once the bugs are found and categorized, it's time to improve them. Depending on the problem, these can be functional or conceptual improvements. It can also happen that you need more or better ideas because none of the prototypes are really convincing. That's the strength of the Design Thinking process. It is a cycle that can be started again and again at any point.

So the second attempt of the prototype is about two questions:

- **How can we solve the problem even better?**

- **How can we improve the known bugs?**

It makes sense that the question of the problem is still before the error. It reminds you that it's still about solving the problem, not just improving the prototype. And sometimes there can be enlightenment during the error improvement process. In Asia, the programmers of an app that transports people with motor rickshaws similar to Uber had been looking for ideas to improve the customers' experience. They wanted to stand out more from the competition and programmed apps as prototypes to order such a motorcycle taxi. One idea was to get the approximate price, a photo of the driver and an SMS if the taxi was close to the pick-up point. They had the users test it, and they were basically thrilled. A woman then wrote, "The driver was so nice and waited until I was really in the house." That was just feedback, not even a mistake. But the potential was immediately recognized, and from then on all drivers were told to wait after 10 o'clock in the evening when they dropped customers off at home until they had safely entered the house. And of course this was also communicated as a special service in the app.

Visualize with Storyboards

After the first tests are finished and you have changed the prototypes accordingly, it can be helpful to work with a storyboard in the next round. The term actually comes from the movie industry, where a script is broken down into different stories. These are then painted on like in a comic book. Such visualization gives the actor and the cameraman a first impression of what the scene should look like but is also helpful to check continuity.

Storyboards in Design Thinking look similar, but they have a different script. The person who is in the center is, of course, the persona. The storyboard tells the story of the persona and how your idea will help her. Like every story, it has a beginning, a middle part and an end.

At the beginning is your persona, who is introduced to the story with her needs and desires. The middle part first describes the environment in which the story takes place, the deep needs of the persona, her pain and suffering as well as the contact points. Then the solutions are introduced and at the end of the story everyone is happy.

A **fictional example** of such **a storyboard** could be:

Inauguration

This is Helga, 62 years old, clerk at the municipal administration, mother of two children, widowed, cat owner, who sings in the choir of the Protestant parish church on the weekend. She is a bank customer, but she does not dare to use cash machines because she is afraid. So, in order to be paid money, she has to go to a branch of her bank every time and wait for it to open.

Middle section

Helga stands at the supermarket checkout and finds that she doesn't have enough cash with her. She was late for the bank yesterday, and now she has to put the detergent back. The saleswoman asks her why she doesn't want to pay with her card. She says that she can't remember the PIN number and was told she shouldn't write it down.

The Solution

The Design Thinking workshops had previously discussed the problem and found that forgetting the PIN is still a big problem for many, especially older, customers. A system was developed that, analogous to that of number flags, converted the numbers into images, for example the two into a swan and the eight into a pretzel, the one into a stick and the zero into an egg. Because we can remember pictures better than numbers, the PIN 2810 in this case would be a swan eating a pretzel, walking on a stick and laying an egg. Such pictures don't have to make sense, only the order is important.

The customer was offered this solution, and she assembled her own picture. So that she didn't forget the picture, she painted it on a piece of paper and put it into her wallet. Since now not the PIN but only a—quasi coded—picture on a note was in the wallet, she was also no longer afraid that someone unauthorized could use it.

The Resolution

With the small piece of paper she was now able to use ATMs even outside bank opening hours and the last picture shows how she pays with the card in the supermarket.

Realization

After several runs of tests and adjustments, at some point the time will have come when the prototype or the idea concept must be turned into something that can actually be implemented. If there are several concepts and prototypes, now is the time to decide on one or two.

Some Design Thinking users see the process as finished when a prototype or concept is developed that satisfactorily solves the problem. The reason is that Design Thinking is seen as a way to produce ideas to solve a problem, not to solve the problem itself. It's also true that the idea is at the forefront, but you can also argue that the creative process continues in the implementation. Some problems can only arise during implementation. One example is the Tesla Company. Founder Elon Musk tested and planned a lot but was surprised to discover that it makes a difference whether you want to build 10 cars or 10,000. The scaling of a production in particular is not linear but often in very strange curves. In principle, the implementation phase is another small loop in Design Thinking that is based on the same methodology—except that in this case the customers are the stakeholders and you have to find ideas to convince them.

In order to be able to implement a new idea, you should first consider whether and how it can fit into the existing structures. Is the canteen even capable of cooking new healthy dishes? Can ATMs simply be converted? What does the company or organization need to implement the idea?

The two big questions that need to be answered during implementation are:

How can I integrate the idea into the running operation?

Which resistances are to be expected?

Since most processes are about changing existing processes, change management comes into play here. You first have to understand what the current processes look like then find a way to implement the idea and then test whether the new or changed process works.

An example from practice: The Austrian Federal Railway has used Design Thinking to improve the customer experience. The toilets were repeatedly addressed in the surveys. These would look like a station toilet, sober, dirty and uninviting. The combination of steel lavatories and grey walls particularly made the toilet a very desolate place. The idea that came up: photo wallpapers showing a forest and scented spray. The advantage of the idea was that it could be quickly upscaled from the prototype. First a toilet was equipped with it and then all trains could be redesigned bit by bit, without any great delays, because the photo wallpapers were cut to the standardized toilet walls and could therefore be glued on in a short time.[11]

In order to implement an idea, you must first make an analysis of the stakeholders. Who is affected by the implementation? In most cases, this is many more people and roles than you might think at first. Here is a list of typical stakeholders:

- department heads

- related customers

---

[11] VIENNA ONLINE (2014): Duftende WCs und Fototapeten in 250 ÖBB-Nahverkehrszügen. URL: http://www.vienna.at/duftende-wcs-und-fototapeten-in-250-oebb-nahverkehrszuegen/4122563 [Date of Reference: 28-04-2018]

- authorities

- accounting department

- lawmakers

- colleagues

- clients

- marketing

- competitor

- potential clients

- product development

- suppliers

This is only a selection because, especially in a company, there can always be certain employees who are fundamentally opposed to new ideas. If you have named all stakeholders, you can start a **Force Field Analysis** and write down which of them are the driving forces and which are the more hindering forces.

The next step is to develop **strategies**, support the driving forces and convince the hindering forces of the idea as far as possible. It makes little sense to give employees freedom of thought for the development of ideas and, as soon as it comes to implementation, implement them with an order from the boss. The more stakeholders on board, the better.

One method is to show the before and after. Here the prototypes can come into play again, as far as they really give a better picture than the actual situation. The more figurative these comparisons are, the more convincing they are. Especially within a company you can also do workshops that deal with the implementation of the idea. If it helps, you can also use storyboards here again.

Caution: A workshop and the finding of ideas may have been so positive and creative that, in the end, there can always be someone who is offended that their own idea was not implemented. Sometimes even the best co-creation attempts won't help. Such people can then become big obstacles in the implementation of ideas. Try to identify them and develop strategies, either to bring them back into the team or to keep their influence as small as possible.

If you know who the stakeholders are, what resistance there can be and how you can resolve it if necessary, then it's the big plan, namely the strategic resources that are needed. The best way to do this is to use a table:

	idea 1	idea 2
Description of the idea		
What are the resources and skills needed to implement it?		
What resources and skills exist?		
Which loopholes exist?		
How can the loopholes be closed?		

In most cases, the problem is finding the right mix of people and technical resources. When it comes to training employees in Asian food in the canteen, someone still has to cook lunch. On the train, you can't close all the toilets at the same time, but you have to make a plan for how this can be done.

The bigger an idea, and the more technical components it has, the more difficult it will be to implement. This is not intended to make the idea obsolete but only to show that you have to think a lot if, for example, you want to change the screens of all ATMs.

One example of how everything can be done in the shortest possible time, if it is well planned, was the changeover to the euro. Here the idea of a new currency had to be implemented within a few days, in some cases within one night. The idea was to convert ATMs but also all other types of machines that process money, such as cigarette machines, ticket machines and gambling machines. This is only an indication that gigantic projects can be successfully implemented (at least as far as the technical side is concerned).

Cost

Cost is a topic that is usually left out of the discussion when it comes to prototypes and the Design Thinking process. One reason for this is that money is extremely inhibiting to creativity. If you are supposed to create ideas but every second idea is dismissed as too expensive, then the process is not much fun and will hardly produce good results.

Design Thinking is about getting a quick solution to a problem with a small budget. It's not so much about getting a cheap solution (unless it's set as a parameter at the beginning of the project, but even then it should be "as cheap as possible" rather than a fixed amount).

In the implementation phase, however, the issue will be money. Therefore, a cost analysis should already be included in the idea description:

- What are the product costs (new food, new screens, photo wallpaper, etc.)?

- What are the personnel costs?

- What other costs are incurred?

- What costs are incurred due to loss of production during implementation?

The goal of cost analysis is not to destroy the idea but to find ways (and funds) to implement it. Design Thinking can also be used here if the budget is not sufficient because this is a problem and a solution has to be found.

Summary

Too often new methods are used only because they are new and because one thinks one has a cure-all. Especially now, when the pressure for companies to innovate is higher than ever before, the executive floors and product developers welcome anything that promises a cure. But Design Thinking is not a healing process. It does not offer a solution but produces solution ideas. Implementing them needs a different decision-making process than finding ideas.

One of the biggest mistakes made in a Design Thinking process is the decision to move there. But that's fundamentally wrong. You saw in the last chapter that it is and must be the stakeholders who make the decision. The Design Thinking team is just a helper who prepares the decision. Project leaders who don't want to take responsibility (and top managers who don't have good ideas themselves and then set up an idea team) often enough want to have a culprit if something goes wrong. But they are also the first to point out that it was their project.

If, on the other hand, you see Design Thinking as a process to drive innovation quickly and cheaply, then you will have a lot of fun with it. One of the reasons teams like to do Design Thinking is because it's so analogous. Many of the phases work best with good, well-tried paper and pens. You can provide these. And even with software processes, the various pages of the software are first painted on paper.

You can get more out of yourself if all your senses are involved. Then you can make more associations. Even if you go out and see and feel and smell the environment your customers are in, you will understand them better than if you try to do this based on the data of your CRM system. And then you and your team will produce great ideas!

Yours,

Kilian Langenfeld

content. Therefore, the Author hereby explicitly distances himself from the content of all linked pages that have been modified after the link was set. For illegal, incorrect or incomplete content and in particular for damages resulting from the use or non-use of this information, the provider of the page in question, but not the Author of this book, is responsible.

Bibliography

Boag, P. (2018): What Is Customer Journey Mapping and How to Start? URL: https://boagworld.com/ usability/customer-journey-mapping/ [Date of Reference: 04-04-2018]

Design Thinking: The Guidebook for Public Sector innovation in Bhutan. URL: http://www.rcsc.gov.bt/ wp-content/ uploads/2017/07/dt-guide-book-master-copy.pdf [Date of Reference: 20-06-2018]

Design for Founders: 10 Powerful Case Studies of Remarkable Business Growth With Design You Need to See. URL: https://www.designforfounders.com/ business-growth-with-design/ [Date of Reference: 29-05-2018]

Design Kit: Methods. URL: http://www.designkit.org/ methods [Date of Reference: 01-06-2018]

Eshaghmohammadi, F. (2016): Become the patient – Design Thinking Grundlagen. URL: http://www.ppcdetective.de/ blog/design-thinking-blog/become-the-patient-design-thinking-grundlagen/ [Date of Reference: 15-05-2018]

Gullberg, G.; Widmark E.; Nyström, M.; Landström, A. (2006): DESIGN THINKING in BUSINESS INNOVATION

International Organization for Standardization (2010): Ergonomics of human-system interaction -- Part 210: Human-centred design for interactive systems

Lanoue, S. (2015): IDEO's 6 Step Human-Centered Design Process: How to Make Things People Want. URL: https://www.usertesting.com/blog/2015/07/09/how-ideo-uses-customer-insights-to-design-innovative-products-users-love/ [Date of Reference: 10-05-2018]

Kramer, A. (2016): Design Thinking in der Praxis: Casinos, MAM, Erste Bank, ÖBB. URL: https://www.trend.at/ branchen/karrieren/design-thinking-praxis-7624507 [Date of Reference: 05-04-2018]

Roland Berger: Design Thinking: Von einer Produktentwicklungsmethode zu einem Ansatz für strategische Entscheidungsprozesse. URL: https://www.rolandberger.com/de/press/Design-Thinking-Von-einer-Produktentwicklungsmethode-zu-einem-Ansatz-f%C3%BCr-strate-2.html [Date of Reference: 20-04-2018]

Russo, B. et al. (2012): Design Thinking Business Innovation, MJV Press, Rio de Janeiro

VIENNA ONLINE (2014): Duftende WCs und Fototapeten in 250 ÖBB-Nahverkehrszügen. URL: http://www.vienna.at/duftende-wcs-und-fototapeten-in-250-oebb-nahverkehrszuegen/4122563 [Date of Reference: 28-04-2018]